RETIREMENT PLANNING GUIDE FOR BEGINNERS

Simple, Smart and Ready for Your Best Years

By

MAXWELL REED

Copyright © 2024 by MAXWELL REED

All rights reserved. No part of this publication may be reproduced, stored or transmitted in any form or by any means, electronic, mechanical, photocopying, recording, scanning, or otherwise without written permission from the publisher. It is illegal to copy this book, post it to a website, or distribute it by any other means without permission, except for brief quotations used in reviews.

TABLE OF CONTENTS

INTRODUCTION 1

THE JOURNEY BEGINS 5
    Understanding Retirement at Any Age 6
    It's Never Too Early (or Too Late!) 8
    Why Most People Get Retirement Wrong 10

WHAT RETIREMENT MEANS TO YOU 14
    Defining Your Perfect Future 15
    Debunking Retirement Myths You've Always Heard ... 17
    How Lifestyle Shapes Your Savings Plan 20

HOW MUCH IS ENOUGH? 23
    Shattering the 'Magic Number' Myth 23
    Setting Realistic Financial Goals 26
    Building a Plan That Fits Your Life 29

BUILDING YOUR RETIREMENT FORTRESS ... 34
    The Power of Compound Interest: Your Best Friend .. 35
    The Art of Diversification: What Really Works 38
    Navigating Through Stocks, Bonds, and Other Investments (Without the Jargon!) 41

YOUR 401(K), IRA, AND BEYOND 46

UNLOCKING HIDDEN TREASURES.......................... 46
    Making the Most of Employer Benefits................... 47
    IRAs: Your Personalized Retirement Vehicle.......... 50
    The Magic of Matching Contributions and Tax Perks. 54

HOW TO DODGE THE BIGGEST MISTAKE.............. 61
    Avoiding the Pitfalls That Sabotage Savings.......... 61
    Recognizing Financial Traps and Learning to Steer Clear.. 63
    The Emotional Side of Retirement Planning: Keeping Stress Out... 66

MAXIMIZING YOUR INCOME STREAMS IN RETIREMENT.. 69
    Social Security Demystified................................... 69
    Passive Income and Alternative Strategies: Thinking Beyond the Obvious... 72
    Building Backup Plans - Safety Nets that Work...... 75

THE TIME FACTOR.. 79
When should you retire?..79
    Early Retirement vs. Delayed Retirement: Pros, Cons, and Surprises.. 80
    The Age Factor: How Timing Affects Your Savings 83
    What to Do When Life Throws a Curveball............. 86

ADJUSTING FOR THE UNKNOWN............................ 90
    Preparing for Healthcare Costs: Reality, Not Scare Tactics... 91

Inflation-Proofing Your Retirement............................93
Handling Unexpected Life Events with Confidence 96

MAKING YOUR MONEY LAST................................. 100
The Exit Strategy... 100

How to Spend Wisely Without Sacrificing Comfort..... 101

Withdrawal Strategies: Stretching Your Savings the Right Way.. 103

Protecting Your Nest Egg: Simple Steps for Longevity.. 107

LIVING YOUR BEST LIFE AFTER RETIREMENT.... 111

How to Create a Lifestyle You'll Love Without Stressing About Money... 112

Thriving in Retirement: Beyond Just Financial Security.. 115

Retirement Isn't the End, It's the Next Adventure. 118

YOUR PERSONALIZED ACTION PLAN....................122
Ready, Set, Retire.. 122

A Step-by-Step Checklist to Get Started Right Away. 123

Sticking to the Plan (And What to Do When You Need to Adjust)... 127

Building Confidence in Your Financial Future....... 130

INTRODUCTION

Retirement. Just the word alone can stir up a mixed bag of emotions. For some, it's the dream of endless vacations, lounging on sun-drenched beaches, or spending more time with family. For others, it's a shadowy concept, something they'll "deal with later," almost like an unsolved riddle waiting at the end of their working years. But what if I told you that retirement is neither the end nor an elusive mystery? What if it could be the start of something you've always wanted but never dared to fully imagine?

You might have picked up this book out of curiosity, or perhaps out of necessity, but whatever led you here, know this: you're not just reading another generic guide filled with numbers and boring jargon. This book is a journey—your journey. And right now, you're standing at the beginning of that path, whether you're in your twenties and retirement feels like a distant concept, or in your fifties wondering if you've saved enough.

But let's forget the anxiety and the complicated spreadsheets for a second. Let's pause. Take a deep breath. This is not a book about getting bogged down with fears or regrets about what you haven't done yet. It's about empowerment. It's about creating your vision for the future, one that fits you perfectly. Because here's the truth: retirement isn't a one-size-fits-all. It's as unique as you are.

You've been told all sorts of things about retirement. Start saving early. Get that magic number. Don't count on Social Security. Invest in this, avoid that. There's so much noise out there that it's easy to feel overwhelmed. But what if retirement planning didn't have to be a struggle? What if it could actually be exciting?

In these pages, I'll break down the complexities of retirement in a way that makes sense. We'll uncover the hidden gems that most people overlook, and together, we'll craft a plan that doesn't just get you through retirement, but helps you thrive in it. Think of this book as your good guide to retirement and instead of dry instructions, it's filled with creative shortcuts, insightful detours, and inspiring views along the way. And it's all laid out in a way that anyone—whether you're 12, 35, or 60—can understand.

No more waiting for the "right time." This is your time. The secret isn't when to start; it's simply that you do start. Right now. Whether you're starting from scratch or already have a few pieces in place, this book will meet you where you are and help you design the future you deserve.

Retirement is no longer a finish line. It's the gateway to your next adventure. And the best part? You get to decide how that adventure unfolds.

So, turn the page. Let's begin.

THE JOURNEY BEGINS

Retirement might feel like something far off in the future, something reserved for a much older version of yourself. But the truth is, the journey toward retirement doesn't begin when you're in your 60s—it starts much earlier. No matter where you are in life right now, the sooner you begin planning, the smoother your path will be. And don't worry if you're late to the party, either. Every step you take now will count.

Retirement planning is not just about saving money, it's about ensuring you have the freedom to live your life on your own terms when the time comes. Whether you're a teenager just starting your first job or someone in their mid-40s trying to make sense of it all, understanding the importance of starting now can make a world of difference.

Understanding Retirement at Any Age

Most people think of retirement planning as something you should only start worrying about when you hit your 40s or 50s. That's a big misconception. The reality is, retirement planning is like planting a tree—the earlier you do it, the stronger it grows. But even if you plant it later, it can still thrive with the right care. So, let's break it down in a way that makes sense no matter how old you are.

If you're young, you've probably got a lot on your mind: education, starting a career, maybe even figuring out what direction you want your life to take. Retirement planning is probably the last thing on your to-do list, but trust me, even a small effort right now can set you up for something big down the road. Imagine being 30 years old and already having a sizable chunk saved up because you started saving as soon as you got your first paycheck at 18. It doesn't take much—just small, regular contributions—and you're already ahead of the game. What makes the journey smoother when you're young is the luxury of time. The power of compound interest is like a magic ingredient that works behind the scenes, multiplying your money as you go about your day-to-day life.

But what if you're not young anymore, and you haven't started planning? Let me reassure you: it's not too late. Sure, the journey might be a little steeper, but that doesn't mean it's impossible. The important thing to remember is that every dollar you save today will benefit you tomorrow. Even if you're in your 40s or 50s, making retirement planning a priority now can still lead to a happy retirement.

Now, if you find yourself approaching retirement age without a clear plan, don't panic. It's easy to feel overwhelmed, but the important thing to remember is that it's never too late to start taking control of your finances, you still have time to make meaningful changes. This could mean ramping up your savings contributions, exploring new investment options, or even delaying retirement to boost your financial security. The key is to take that first step—acknowledge where you are and make a plan to move forward.

It's Never Too Early (or Too Late!)

When it comes to retirement planning, timing is everything. Many people mistakenly believe that they need to be in a certain place in life before they can start saving for retirement. The truth is that it's never too early—or too late—to start planning. Each stage of your life presents unique opportunities to make decisions that will benefit you in the long run.

If you're just starting your career, consider this: every dollar you save now can significantly impact your future. Even if you can only set aside a small amount each month, it will add up over time. This is where the concept of compound interest comes into play. Essentially, compound interest means that the interest you earn on your savings begins to generate its own interest. Over the years, this can lead to exponential growth in your savings. So, don't be discouraged if you can't save a lot right away. Starting small can lead to big results down the line.

But what if you're already past that early stage? Perhaps you're in your thirties or forties and feeling like you've missed the boat on retirement savings. Rest assured, it's not too late. Many people in this age group are in a better position to save than they realize. If you're earning a stable income and your expenses are manageable, consider ramping up your retirement contributions. This could mean maxing out your employer-sponsored retirement plans or exploring additional investment opportunities like Roth IRAs.

It's also important to recognize that life changes, such as marriage, divorce, or having children, can impact your retirement strategy. If you find yourself navigating these transitions, take the time to evaluate your financial situation and adjust your plans accordingly. The beauty of retirement planning is that it's flexible. It can adapt to your life circumstances, so don't hesitate to revisit your goals and make necessary changes.

For those nearing retirement age, it's easy to feel like time is running out. You may be worried about not having enough saved up, but remember: every step you take now can make a difference. Consider delaying retirement for a few years to give your savings more time to grow. Or explore ways to cut expenses and redirect those funds toward your retirement savings. It's all about finding the right balance and making informed decisions that align with your goals.

Why Most People Get Retirement Wrong

Despite the wealth of information available on retirement planning, many people still find themselves unprepared for this crucial life stage. So, why do so many people get retirement wrong? One of the biggest pitfalls is the tendency to underestimate the amount of money needed to retire comfortably. Many individuals think they can rely solely on Social Security benefits, but this often falls short of covering living expenses. It's essential to take a realistic look at your financial needs in retirement and plan accordingly.

Another common mistake is procrastination. Life is busy, and it's easy to push retirement planning to the back burner, thinking there will be plenty of time to figure it out later. However, the longer you wait, the harder it becomes to catch up. Delaying your savings means missing out on valuable years of compound interest, and those lost years can add up to a significant amount of money over time.

Additionally, many people fail to take advantage of employer-sponsored retirement plans, such as 401(k)s, which often come with matching contributions. This is essentially free money that can dramatically boost your savings. Not contributing to these plans is like leaving money on the table. It's important to understand the benefits of these accounts and make the most of them as part of your retirement strategy.

Lastly, a lack of financial literacy can lead to poor retirement decisions. Many individuals are unfamiliar with investment options, savings strategies, or how to create a diversified portfolio. This can result in missed opportunities and costly mistakes. It's crucial to educate yourself about retirement planning, whether through books, online resources, or even consulting a financial advisor. The more you know, the better equipped you'll be to make informed decisions that align with your goals.

As you embark on your retirement planning journey, remember that it's a process—one that requires careful consideration and proactive steps. By understanding the importance of starting now, embracing the flexibility of your timeline, and avoiding common pitfalls, you'll be well on your way to a successful and fulfilling retirement. This journey is about more than just numbers; it's about crafting a life you love, filled with experiences and opportunities. So take a deep breath, set your intentions, and begin your journey toward a secure and joyful retirement.

The best time to start was yesterday; the next best time is now.

WHAT RETIREMENT MEANS TO YOU

Retirement is a concept that evokes a wide array of emotions and ideas, often varying significantly from one person to another. For some, it symbolizes a long-awaited freedom from the daily grind of work, while for others, it may represent uncertainty or anxiety about the future. Understanding what retirement truly means to you is a crucial step in the planning process. It's essential to recognize that retirement isn't a one-size-fits-all experience; instead, it's a deeply personal journey shaped by your aspirations, values, and lifestyle choices. This section will explore how to define your perfect retirement future, debunk common myths that might be clouding your perception, and highlight how your lifestyle influences your savings plan.

Defining Your Perfect Future

When we think about retirement, it's important to start by asking ourselves: what does it look like for me? The answer can vary greatly based on individual preferences, dreams, and life circumstances. For some, retirement might mean traveling the world, exploring new cultures, and tasting exotic foods. For others, it could mean settling into a cozy home, surrounded by family and friends, and pursuing hobbies they've always put on hold due to work commitments. There's no right or wrong answer; it's about defining what truly resonates with you.

Start by visualizing your ideal retirement scenario. What activities do you want to engage in? Do you see yourself volunteering, gardening, or starting a small business? Perhaps you envision spending more time with grandchildren, taking art classes, or simply enjoying quiet evenings reading books. Take some time to reflect on your interests and passions. Write down your thoughts. This exercise will help you gain clarity about what you want to achieve in your retirement years.

Additionally, consider your values. What is most important to you? Is it security, adventure, community, or personal fulfillment? Understanding your core values can significantly influence how you envision your retirement. For example, if community engagement is vital to you, you might want to prioritize living in a neighborhood where you can connect with others and participate in local activities. Alternatively, if adventure is your driving force, you might choose a retirement plan that allocates funds for travel and exploration.

It's also essential to acknowledge that retirement can change as you age. Your dreams and desires may evolve, so it's crucial to stay adaptable. What you envision for your retirement in your 50s may differ from your vision in your 70s or beyond. That's okay! The key is to regularly reassess your goals and make adjustments as needed. This flexibility allows you to create a retirement plan that aligns with your evolving aspirations, ultimately leading to a more fulfilling experience.

Debunking Retirement Myths You've Always Heard

Retirement is often surrounded by myths and misconceptions that can skew our understanding and planning efforts. Let's take a moment to debunk some of these common retirement myths that may have lingered in your mind, preventing you from approaching retirement with confidence and clarity.

One prevalent myth is the idea that retirement means you'll have nothing to do. Many people envision retirement as a period filled with boredom and inactivity. However, the reality is quite the opposite. Retirement can be a time of vibrant engagement, exploration, and personal growth. It's a chance to pursue interests and hobbies you might have set aside during your working years. The key is to proactively create a fulfilling retirement lifestyle that keeps you mentally and physically active. Whether it's joining clubs, taking classes, or engaging in volunteer work, the options are endless.

Another common misconception is that you will need to drastically reduce your spending once you retire. While it's true that some expenses may decrease—such as commuting costs or work-related expenses—others may rise. Healthcare costs, for instance, can become a significant factor in your retirement budget. Additionally, you may want to travel more or pursue new hobbies that come with their own costs. Instead of assuming you'll need to cut your spending significantly, focus on creating a realistic budget that reflects your desired lifestyle in retirement.

There's also the belief that Social Security will cover all your retirement needs. While Social Security can provide a valuable safety net, it's not enough to rely on as your sole source of income. Many people find that their Social Security benefits cover only a portion of their expenses in retirement. It's crucial to have additional savings and investment strategies in place to ensure you can maintain your desired standard of living.

Finally, some people think they can't afford to retire early or take time off. This myth can lead to unnecessary stress and a reluctance to plan for a fulfilling retirement. The truth is that with careful planning and smart financial decisions, it is possible to retire early or enjoy periods of sabbatical throughout your career. The key is to create a savings plan that aligns with your goals and priorities. This might involve making sacrifices early on, but the payoff can be well worth it in the long run.

By debunking these myths, you can approach retirement with a fresh perspective and a more realistic understanding of what to expect. Remember that retirement is a personal journey, and it's up to you to define what it means for you, free from the misconceptions that often cloud our judgment.

How Lifestyle Shapes Your Savings Plan

Your lifestyle plays a crucial role in shaping your retirement savings plan. The choices you make today about your living situation, spending habits, and career trajectory will directly impact how much you'll need to save for retirement. Understanding this relationship is vital for creating a successful retirement strategy that aligns with your unique goals and circumstances.

First, consider your current lifestyle. Are you someone who enjoys a minimalist lifestyle, or do you tend to indulge in luxury? Your spending habits now can significantly affect your savings for the future. If you find yourself living paycheck to paycheck or consistently overspending on non-essential items, it's crucial to reassess your financial priorities. Implementing a budget can help you identify areas where you can cut back, allowing you to redirect those funds toward retirement savings. It's about striking a balance between enjoying your present and investing in your future.

Next, think about your desired lifestyle in retirement. This is where your earlier reflections on your perfect future come into play. How do you want to live? Will you want to travel extensively? Will you be supporting a family member or pursuing hobbies that require financial investment? The more clarity you have about your future lifestyle, the more accurately you can calculate how much you'll need to save.

For instance, if your dream retirement involves frequent travel and exploration, it's essential to budget for those experiences. Consider setting specific savings goals for travel-related expenses, and factor those into your overall retirement plan. On the other hand, if you envision a quieter retirement filled with local activities and community involvement, your savings goals might be different.

Additionally, your career path can influence your savings strategy. If you're in a high-paying profession, you may have the potential to save more aggressively. Conversely, if you're in a lower-paying field, you might need to explore alternative savings strategies or side hustles to supplement your income. It's essential to assess your earning potential and identify opportunities for advancement that can bolster your retirement savings.

Finally, as you evaluate your lifestyle, consider the importance of health and well-being. Living a healthy lifestyle can lead to lower healthcare costs in retirement, which can significantly impact your savings. Investing in your physical and mental well-being now can pay off in the long run, allowing you to enjoy a longer, healthier retirement. Consider incorporating exercise, nutritious eating, and stress-reduction techniques into your daily routine to foster a healthier lifestyle.

Remember that this journey is not just about financial security; it's about creating a life that aligns with your passions and values. As you pass through this exciting phase, stay open to new possibilities and remain proactive in pursuing the retirement of your dreams. Your future self will thank you for it.

HOW MUCH IS ENOUGH?

When it comes to retirement planning, one of the most frequently asked questions is, "How much do I need to retire?" This question can evoke anxiety, confusion, and sometimes a sense of hopelessness. Many people chase after a so-called "magic number," believing that if they just save a specific amount, they will be secure and happy in retirement. However, this notion can lead to unrealistic expectations and missed opportunities for financial peace. In this section, we will explore the myth of the magic number, discuss how to set realistic financial goals tailored to your unique situation, and help you build a retirement plan that fits seamlessly into your life.

Shattering the 'Magic Number' Myth

The idea of a magic number in retirement planning often stems from generalized advice and statistical data that attempt to quantify what individuals should have saved by a certain age. This figure typically represents a lump sum that many financial experts suggest—often ranging from 10 to 25 times your annual income. While these guidelines can serve as a helpful starting point, they can also be misleading. The reality is that the concept of a single magic number is overly simplistic and fails to consider the nuances of individual lifestyles, expenses, and goals.

One reason the magic number myth is so problematic is that it can create an unrealistic benchmark for people. Many individuals may believe that once they reach this magical sum, they can finally relax and enjoy their retirement. However, retirement is not just about how much money you have; it's about how effectively you manage your finances to support your desired lifestyle. The amount of money you need in retirement depends on various factors, including your age, health, retirement age, income needs, and life expectancy.

Instead of fixating on a specific dollar amount, it's essential to focus on your unique financial situation and retirement goals. Start by considering what you want your retirement to look like. What are your interests? Will you travel frequently? Do you plan to live in a particular location? Will you continue to work part-time? By answering these questions, you can create a more tailored plan that considers your specific needs rather than a one-size-fits-all magic number.

Moreover, it's essential to recognize that inflation will play a significant role in your retirement planning. The cost of living can change drastically over time, which means your expenses today may not reflect what you will need in the future. As prices rise, your savings will need to keep pace to maintain your desired standard of living. Consequently, it's important to build a flexible savings strategy that can adapt to economic changes and inflation.

Ultimately, the magic number myth can lead to feelings of inadequacy if you feel you are falling short of that arbitrary figure. Instead, cultivate a mindset focused on your unique financial journey, allowing for adjustments and flexibility along the way. By shattering this myth, you empower yourself to create a more authentic and fulfilling retirement plan that resonates with your values and goals.

Setting Realistic Financial Goals

Now that we've discussed the pitfalls of the magic number, it's time to focus on setting realistic financial goals that align with your retirement vision. This process involves a careful assessment of your current financial situation, future aspirations, and the lifestyle you wish to achieve during retirement.

The first step in setting realistic financial goals is to assess your current financial health. Take a close look at your income, expenses, savings, and debts. Create a comprehensive budget that outlines your monthly spending habits and helps you identify areas where you can cut back or save more. Knowing your financial landscape is essential for creating achievable retirement goals.

Next, determine your retirement income needs. Consider how much money you will need to maintain your desired lifestyle. Think about your essential expenses, such as housing, healthcare, food, and transportation, as well as discretionary spending on travel, entertainment, and hobbies. Estimating these costs will provide a clearer picture of the income you need during retirement.

Once you have a grasp of your income needs, think about potential sources of retirement income. This may include Social Security benefits, pension plans, retirement accounts, and investments. Understanding your income sources will help you gauge how much you need to save to fill any gaps.

When setting financial goals, aim for a mix of short-term and long-term objectives. Short-term goals could include building an emergency fund, paying off high-interest debt, or contributing to a retirement account. Long-term goals may encompass reaching a specific savings milestone or building a diversified investment portfolio. By establishing both types of goals, you create a balanced financial roadmap that allows for flexibility and growth.

Another vital aspect of setting realistic financial goals is creating a timeline. Consider when you plan to retire and work backward to determine how much you need to save each year to reach your desired income. By breaking down your goals into manageable steps, you can measure your progress over time and make adjustments as necessary.

Furthermore, it's essential to remain adaptable in your goal-setting approach. Life can be unpredictable, and circumstances may change. Reassess your goals regularly to ensure they still align with your evolving lifestyle and retirement vision. By remaining flexible and open to change, you can navigate obstacles with confidence and adjust your financial strategy as needed.

Ultimately, setting realistic financial goals is about creating a personalized plan that reflects your values, aspirations, and circumstances. By taking a holistic approach to your financial future, you empower yourself to make informed decisions and work toward a fulfilling retirement.

Building a Plan That Fits Your Life

Now that you have a clear understanding of your retirement vision and realistic financial goals, it's time to build a plan that fits your life. A successful retirement plan is not just about how much you save but also about how you allocate your resources and manage your finances over time. Let's explore the key components of creating a retirement plan that aligns with your unique needs and aspirations.

The first step in building your retirement plan is to determine your savings strategy. This involves choosing the right retirement accounts and investment options based on your goals, risk tolerance, and time horizon. Consider tax-advantaged retirement accounts, such as a 401(k) or an IRA, as these can provide valuable benefits for long-term savings. Contribute enough to receive any employer match if you have access to a workplace retirement plan, as this can significantly boost your savings.

As you develop your investment strategy, it's essential to consider your risk tolerance. This refers to how comfortable you are with market fluctuations and potential losses. A younger individual may be more inclined to take on higher risk for greater potential rewards, while someone nearing retirement might prioritize capital preservation. Diversifying your investments can help mitigate risk while maximizing potential returns.

Next, ensure your plan includes an emergency fund. This safety net will help you weather unexpected financial challenges that may arise during your retirement years. Aim to have three to six months' worth of living expenses set aside in a high-yield savings account. This fund will provide peace of mind and reduce the need to tap into your retirement savings for unforeseen expenses.

Additionally, consider incorporating insurance options into your retirement plan. Health insurance, long-term care insurance, and life insurance can play critical roles in safeguarding your financial future. Understand the different types of insurance available and assess your needs based on your health status, family history, and retirement plans.

As you implement your plan, stay committed to regularly monitoring and adjusting it as needed. This may involve revisiting your goals, reallocating investments, or increasing contributions based on your financial situation. Life changes—such as a new job, marriage, or unexpected expenses—may necessitate updates to your plan. Establish a routine for reviewing your progress, at least annually, to ensure you're on track toward your retirement objectives.

It's also helpful to seek guidance from financial professionals when building your retirement plan. Financial advisors can provide personalized insights and strategies to help you navigate the complexities of retirement planning. Look for advisors who align with your values and have a fiduciary duty to act in your best interest. A trusted advisor can help you clarify your goals, refine your strategy, and provide accountability as you work toward your retirement.

Lastly, remember that retirement planning is a journey, not a destination. It requires ongoing effort, dedication, and a willingness to adapt. Embrace the process and stay engaged with your finances. Celebrate milestones along the way and acknowledge the progress you've made. The more proactive you are in managing your retirement plan, the more empowered you will feel as you approach this exciting chapter of your life.

Embrace the journey and take proactive steps toward a retirement that brings you joy and satisfaction. Your future self will thank you for the thoughtful planning and effort you invest today.

BUILDING YOUR RETIREMENT FORTRESS

As you embark on your journey toward a secure and fulfilling retirement, it's essential to build a solid financial foundation that can withstand the tests of time and market fluctuations. This foundation—often referred to as your retirement fortress—combines various strategies, tools, and principles designed to maximize your wealth and ensure your financial independence. In this section, we will look into the powerful role of compound interest, explore the art of diversification, and demystify the world of stocks, bonds, and other investments without drowning in jargon. Each of these components will help fortify your retirement strategy, empowering you to navigate the financial landscape with confidence.

The Power of Compound Interest: Your Best Friend

Imagine planting a tree. In the beginning, it's just a small seed buried in the ground. With time, water, sunlight, and care, that seed transforms into a flourishing tree, eventually providing shade and fruit. This process mirrors the concept of compound interest in retirement savings. It's the growth of your money, not just from your contributions but also from the interest your investments earn over time. Understanding and harnessing this power can be a game-changer in your financial journey.

At its core, compound interest means that the interest you earn on your savings also earns interest. This creates a snowball effect; over time, your money can grow exponentially. The earlier you start saving and investing, the more time you give your money to compound. Think of it this way: if you invest $1,000 today with a hypothetical annual interest rate of 5%, in 20 years, you will have approximately $2,653. But if you wait ten years to invest the same amount, you will only have around $1,645 after 20 years. The difference? Time, which allows your money to work for you.

This power of compounding can often be underestimated, especially by younger individuals who may feel retirement is a distant concern. The truth is, the sooner you begin your savings journey, the more significant the impact will be. Each dollar you invest early on has the potential to grow into much more by the time you retire. This principle emphasizes the importance of starting early and contributing consistently, even if the amounts seem small. A little goes a long way when given the chance to compound over time.

It's also crucial to remain invested during market fluctuations. While it's natural to feel anxious during economic downturns, remember that compound interest works best when you stay the course. Selling investments during a market dip can hinder your growth potential. Instead, view market dips as opportunities to buy more at a lower price. Over time, the market tends to rebound, allowing your investments to regain value and continue compounding.

Finally, consider using tax-advantaged accounts like a 401(k) or an IRA to maximize your compounding potential. Contributions to these accounts often grow tax-deferred, meaning you won't owe taxes on your investment gains until you withdraw the money in retirement. This feature enhances the compounding effect, allowing you to keep more of your money working for you over time.

In summary, the power of compound interest is a formidable ally in your retirement planning. By starting early, investing consistently, and allowing your money to grow over time, you can create a strong financial future that supports your dreams and aspirations. Your journey toward building a retirement fortress begins with this powerful concept—your best friend in the world of finance.

The Art of Diversification: What Really Works

When it comes to building your retirement fortress, diversification is a cornerstone strategy that can help you manage risk and optimize your returns. At its essence, diversification involves spreading your investments across various asset classes—such as stocks, bonds, and real estate—to minimize the impact of any single investment's poor performance on your overall portfolio. Let's dive deeper into the art of diversification and explore how it works and why it's essential for your financial future.

Imagine you're at a potluck dinner with friends. If you only bring one dish and it turns out to be a flop, your meal options might be severely limited. However, if you bring several dishes, you can ensure a more enjoyable meal, regardless of any single dish's success. The same principle applies to investing. By diversifying your portfolio, you can reduce the risk associated with any individual investment while enhancing your chances of achieving favorable returns.

One key reason diversification works is that different asset classes often perform differently under various market conditions. For instance, during economic growth, stocks may thrive as companies see increased profits. Conversely, during economic downturns, bonds may outperform stocks as investors seek safer havens for their money. By holding a mix of assets, you can buffer your portfolio against market volatility and improve the likelihood of steady growth over time.

When constructing a diversified portfolio, consider including a mix of domestic and international stocks, bonds, and other assets. Each of these categories can behave differently based on economic conditions, interest rates, and global events. Additionally, you may want to explore alternative investments, such as real estate or commodities, to further broaden your exposure.

Another critical aspect of diversification is regularly rebalancing your portfolio. As markets fluctuate, the proportions of your investments may drift from your desired allocation. For example, if your stock investments outperform the market, they may become a larger percentage of your portfolio than you intended. Rebalancing involves selling some of your top-performing assets and reallocating the proceeds into underperforming ones to maintain your target allocation. This process helps ensure that you're not overly exposed to any single investment or asset class, allowing you to manage risk effectively.

While diversification is a powerful strategy, it's essential to remember that it does not guarantee profits or protect against losses in a declining market. However, it does provide a more balanced approach to investing, which can help you navigate through the ups and downs of the market with greater confidence.

Finally, consider your personal risk tolerance when diversifying. Each individual has different comfort levels regarding risk and potential loss. Assess your financial goals, investment horizon, and emotional response to market fluctuations to determine an appropriate mix of assets for your portfolio. Understanding your risk tolerance will empower you to make informed decisions and create a well-rounded investment strategy that suits your needs.

To round it up, the art of diversification is a powerful tool in building your retirement fortress. By spreading your investments across various asset classes and regularly rebalancing your portfolio, you can manage risk while positioning yourself for potential growth. This strategy will not only enhance your chances of reaching your retirement goals but also provide you with peace of mind as you find your way through the ever-changing terrain of the financial markets.

Navigating Through Stocks, Bonds, and Other Investments (Without the Jargon!)

Navigating the world of investments can sometimes feel overwhelming, especially with the jargon and complex terms often thrown around. However, understanding the basics of stocks, bonds, and other investment vehicles is crucial for building your retirement fortress. By demystifying these concepts and breaking them down into digestible pieces, you'll feel more empowered to make informed decisions about your financial future.

Let's start with stocks. When you purchase a stock, you're buying a small ownership stake in a company. As the company grows and becomes more profitable, the value of your stock may increase, allowing you to sell it for a profit. Additionally, some companies pay dividends—regular cash payments to shareholders—providing another way to earn income from your investment. However, it's important to recognize that stocks can be volatile, meaning their value can fluctuate significantly over time. While investing in stocks can offer the potential for higher returns, it also comes with increased risk.

On the other hand, bonds represent a loan that you make to a government or corporation in exchange for periodic interest payments. When you buy a bond, you're essentially lending your money to the issuer for a specified period. At the end of that period, the issuer repays the principal amount of the bond. Bonds tend to be less volatile than stocks, making them a popular choice for those seeking stability in their investment portfolio. However, they generally offer lower returns compared to stocks, which is why they are often viewed as a safer option.

In addition to stocks and bonds, there are other investment vehicles to consider. Real estate, for example, can be a valuable asset in your retirement portfolio. Investing in real estate can generate rental income while also appreciating in value over time. Real estate investment trusts (REITs) allow you to invest in real estate without the need to buy and manage properties directly. These trusts pool funds from multiple investors to purchase income-producing properties, providing a way to benefit from real estate's potential without the complexities of direct ownership.

Mutual funds and exchange-traded funds (ETFs) are additional investment options that can simplify your portfolio management. These funds pool money from multiple investors to invest in a diversified mix of stocks, bonds, or other assets. By investing in a mutual fund or ETF, you gain exposure to a variety of investments, reducing the risks associated with individual stocks or bonds. They are an excellent option for beginners who want to achieve diversification without having to research and manage numerous investments.

As you explore different investment options, it's essential to develop an investment strategy that aligns with your financial goals and risk tolerance. This strategy will guide your decisions on which investments to pursue and how to allocate your assets effectively. Remember that investing is a long-term journey, and it's essential to remain patient and disciplined throughout the process.

Finally, don't be afraid to seek guidance when finding your way with investing. Financial advisors and online resources can provide valuable insights and help you make informed decisions. Educating yourself about investment options and market trends will empower you to take charge of your financial future.

By understanding the basics of these investment vehicles and how they fit into your retirement strategy, you can make informed choices that align with your financial goals. Remember that building your retirement fortress requires time, patience, and a commitment to learning. By embracing this journey, you'll be well on your way to achieving the secure and fulfilling retirement

YOUR 401(K), IRA, AND BEYOND

UNLOCKING HIDDEN TREASURES

Retirement planning can feel like a long and winding road, but along the way, there are hidden treasures—like your 401(k), IRA, and other savings vehicles—that can make the journey smoother and more rewarding. These tools are not just essential for securing your future; they also offer unique opportunities to grow your wealth, take advantage of tax benefits, and even gain free money through matching contributions. By unlocking the potential of these treasures, you'll give yourself a head start on the path to financial independence. Let's explore how to maximize these benefits in a way that will leave you feeling empowered and ready to take on your retirement goals.

Making the Most of Employer Benefits

One of the greatest perks of working for an employer is the array of benefits that can help you prepare for retirement. Whether it's a 401(k) plan, matching contributions, or profit-sharing, these employer-provided benefits can be like buried treasure—waiting to be discovered and maximized for your long-term advantage. Understanding how to make the most of these benefits is key to building a strong retirement foundation.

Let's start with the 401(k), one of the most common retirement savings plans offered by employers. A 401(k) allows you to save for retirement by contributing a portion of your pre-tax income directly into an investment account. The beauty of this plan lies in its simplicity—your employer typically handles the logistics, and you can set up automatic payroll deductions to make saving effortless. What's more, many employers offer a match on your contributions, meaning they'll contribute additional funds to your account based on what you contribute. For example, if your employer offers a 100% match on the first 5% of your salary that you contribute, and you earn $50,000 annually, you could receive an additional $2,500 each year simply by contributing $2,500 of your own money. That's essentially free money for your retirement!

Maximizing this matching benefit is crucial. If you're not contributing enough to get the full match, you're essentially leaving money on the table. While it might seem challenging to part with a chunk of your paycheck, the long-term benefits far outweigh the short-term sacrifice. Matching contributions accelerate the growth of your retirement savings, giving your nest egg a significant boost over time.

Additionally, 401(k) contributions lower your taxable income in the year you make them. Since contributions are made with pre-tax dollars, they reduce the amount of income subject to federal income tax. This dual benefit—growing your savings while reducing your tax liability—makes a

401(k) one of the most powerful tools in your retirement arsenal.

But it's not just about contributing; it's also about managing your investments wisely. Most 401(k) plans offer a range of investment options, including mutual funds, target-date funds, and bond funds. Take the time to review your options and choose investments that align with your retirement timeline and risk tolerance. If you're not comfortable making these decisions on your own, many plans offer the option to consult with a financial advisor or use automated investment services.

In addition to the 401(k), some employers offer profit-sharing plans or stock options. These programs allow you to share in the company's success by receiving a portion of the profits or purchasing company stock at a discounted rate. While these benefits can provide an excellent boost to your retirement savings, be cautious about over-investing in your employer's stock. Diversification is key to managing risk, so make sure you're not putting too many eggs in one basket.

To truly make the most of your employer benefits, start by contributing enough to your 401(k) to get the full match, review and adjust your investment options periodically, and take advantage of any additional perks like profit-sharing or stock options. By doing so, you'll be well on your way to unlocking the hidden treasures that your employer provides.

IRAs: Your Personalized Retirement Vehicle

While employer-sponsored plans like the 401(k) are powerful tools, they're not the only option for saving for retirement. Individual Retirement Accounts (IRAs) offer a more personalized approach to retirement savings, giving you greater control over how and where your money is invested. Whether you're self-employed, don't have access to a 401(k), or simply want to supplement your savings, an IRA can be a valuable addition to your retirement strategy.

There are two main types of IRAs: Traditional IRAs and Roth IRAs. Each offers distinct advantages, and the right choice for you will depend on your current financial situation and long-term goals. Let's break down the key differences so you can choose the best option for your needs.

A Traditional IRA functions much like a 401(k) in that your contributions are made with pre-tax dollars, which lowers your taxable income for the year. The money in your account grows tax-deferred, meaning you won't owe taxes on the earnings until you begin making withdrawals in retirement. This is a significant advantage if you expect to be in a lower tax bracket when you retire, as you'll pay less in taxes when you withdraw the funds.

On the other hand, a Roth IRA is funded with after-tax dollars. This means you don't get an immediate tax break on your contributions, but your withdrawals in retirement are completely tax-free. This can be an excellent option if you anticipate being in a higher tax bracket when you retire, or if you simply want to ensure that you won't owe taxes on your investment gains down the road. One of the most appealing features of the Roth IRA is that it allows your money to grow tax-free, making it an ideal choice for younger savers with a long investment horizon.

IRAs also offer more flexibility than employer-sponsored plans. While 401(k)s typically have a limited menu of investment options, IRAs allow you to invest in a wide range of assets, including stocks, bonds, mutual funds, and even alternative investments like real estate or cryptocurrency (depending on the provider). This freedom gives you the opportunity to tailor your investments to your specific goals and risk tolerance.

In terms of contribution limits, IRAs have lower annual limits than 401(k)s. For 2024, the maximum contribution to an IRA is $6,500 (or $7,500 if you're age 50 or older). While this is less than what you can contribute to a 401(k), it's still a significant amount that can grow substantially over time, especially if you take advantage of the tax benefits each type of IRA offers.

If you're self-employed or a small business owner, you might also consider a SEP IRA or a Solo 401(k). These plans offer higher contribution limits and are designed to help entrepreneurs and small business owners save for retirement in a tax-advantaged way. A SEP IRA allows you to contribute up to 25% of your compensation, with a maximum of $66,000 for 2024. Meanwhile, a Solo 401(k) offers similar benefits but allows you to contribute both as an employee and an employer, potentially increasing your contribution limit.

Ultimately, an IRA offers a flexible and personalized retirement vehicle that can complement your employer-sponsored plan or serve as your primary savings tool. Whether you choose a Traditional or Roth IRA, or explore specialized options like a SEP IRA or Solo 401(k), these accounts provide valuable opportunities to grow your retirement savings in a tax-advantaged manner.

The Magic of Matching Contributions and Tax Perks

Let's take a moment to appreciate the magic that is matching contributions and tax perks. These two elements are like the secret sauce in your retirement recipe—adding flavor, richness, and a little extra something to make your savings strategy truly shine.

Matching contributions are one of the most powerful tools in your retirement toolkit, and they're essentially free money. We touched on this earlier with the 401(k), but let's dig a little deeper into how matching works and why it's so important to maximize this benefit. Many employers will match a percentage of your contributions to your retirement plan, effectively doubling (or at least significantly boosting) your savings. If your employer offers a 100% match on contributions up to 5% of your salary, and you contribute that 5%, your savings are instantly doubled. Even if your employer only offers a partial match, such as 50% up to 6%, that's still extra money going straight into your retirement account.

Why is this so magical? Because matching contributions accelerate the growth of your retirement savings without requiring any extra effort on your part. It's like getting a raise that goes directly into your future, and the more you contribute, the more your employer may match. Failing to take full advantage of this benefit is essentially leaving money on the table—money that could be compounding and growing over the years to give you a more secure retirement.

The magic doesn't stop with matching contributions. The tax perks associated with retirement accounts are another crucial element that can significantly enhance your savings. Depending on whether you're contributing to a Traditional or Roth IRA (or a 401(k)), you'll either lower your taxable income now or enjoy tax-free withdrawals later.

For example, with a Traditional 401(k) or IRA, your contributions are made with pre-tax dollars, meaning you don't pay taxes on the money you contribute until you withdraw it in retirement. This reduces your taxable income in the year you make the contribution, potentially lowering your tax bill. This immediate tax break is incredibly helpful, especially for those in higher tax brackets. On the flip side, with a Roth 401(k) or IRA, your contributions are made with after-tax dollars, but the magic happens when you retire—your withdrawals, including all the investment earnings, are completely tax-free.

Both options offer valuable tax advantages, and choosing the right one depends on your financial situation and future expectations. If you anticipate being in a lower tax bracket when you retire, a Traditional account might be more beneficial, allowing you to defer taxes until later. If you expect to be in a higher tax bracket in retirement, a Roth account could be the better option, as you'll enjoy tax-free withdrawals when you may need it most.

Another key benefit of both types of accounts is tax-deferred growth. Whether you have a Traditional or Roth retirement account, the investments within these accounts grow without being subject to capital gains taxes each year. This means that as your investments increase in value over time, you won't be taxed on those gains as they happen. Instead, the money stays in the account, compounding year after year, building up your wealth more quickly than if you were taxed on your gains annually. This tax-deferred growth is especially powerful over long periods, allowing your money to work harder for you.

Now, what happens when you take full advantage of both matching contributions and the tax perks? The result is exponential growth in your retirement savings. Consider the example of a 401(k) with a company match and pre-tax contributions. Each year, you not only contribute your own money (which grows tax-deferred), but your employer adds to that amount with their match. Plus, the money you contribute reduces your taxable income, giving you an immediate tax break. Over time, this combination creates a powerful engine of compound growth that can supercharge your retirement savings.

For those with access to both employer-sponsored retirement accounts and IRAs, there's another level of magic to consider. By contributing to both types of accounts, you can take advantage of the unique benefits each offers. Maxing out your 401(k) contributions to get the full employer match, and then contributing to an IRA (either Traditional or Roth, depending on your situation) allows you to diversify your retirement savings vehicles and tax advantages. This multi-pronged approach ensures that you're maximizing your retirement potential and positioning yourself for a comfortable and secure future.

It's also important to keep in mind the IRS contribution limits for both employer-sponsored plans and IRAs. For 2024, the contribution limit for 401(k) plans is $23,000, with an additional $7,500 catch-up contribution allowed for those aged 50 and older. For IRAs, the contribution limit is $6,500, with a $1,000 catch-up contribution for those 50 and older. Understanding these limits and planning accordingly allows you to make the most of your retirement accounts each year.

In the end, the magic of matching contributions and tax perks lies in their ability to help you save more with less effort. By contributing consistently and taking full advantage of these benefits, you'll create a powerful, growing pool of resources that will be there for you when you're ready to retire. Whether it's the immediate benefit of lower taxes today or the long-term benefit of tax-free growth in retirement, these perks make all the difference in helping you build a retirement plan that works for you.

As you navigate through the process of saving for retirement, remember that each contribution—whether it's your own money or a match from your employer—adds up over time. The tax benefits, whether immediate or deferred, enhance your savings in ways that may not be immediately obvious, but will have a huge impact on your financial future. By unlocking these hidden treasures and taking full advantage of the tools at your disposal, you'll be well on your way to building the retirement of your dreams.

HOW TO DODGE THE BIGGEST MISTAKE

Retirement planning is one of the most important financial journeys you'll ever take. It's a path filled with opportunities, but it's also riddled with potential pitfalls that can derail your best-laid plans. The good news is that with some foresight, knowledge, and a few key strategies, you can avoid the common mistakes that many fall into. This section is about learning how to dodge these mistakes before they become obstacles in your road to financial security.

Avoiding the Pitfalls That Sabotage Savings

One of the biggest mistakes people make when saving for retirement is not saving enough or waiting too long to start. It's easy to get caught up in the demands of everyday life—paying off debt, buying a home, raising kids—and put retirement savings on the back burner. But every year that goes by without contributing to your retirement accounts is a missed opportunity for your money to grow. The earlier you start, the more time compound interest has to work its magic.

But it's not just about starting early—it's also about consistency. Some people start strong, then fizzle out, contributing sporadically to their retirement accounts. This can be just as damaging as not saving at all. Think of it this way: saving for retirement is like planting a tree. The more consistent you are in watering it, the stronger and taller it grows over time. Even if you can only afford small contributions at first, those steady, ongoing investments will pay off in the long run.

Another major pitfall is withdrawing from retirement accounts too early. Life can throw curveballs, and it might be tempting to dip into your 401(k) or IRA to cover unexpected expenses. But early withdrawals come with penalties and taxes that can erode your hard-earned savings. Plus, you'll miss out on the future growth that money would have provided. Instead, it's better to build up an emergency fund outside of your retirement accounts to cover those surprises, leaving your nest egg untouched.

Lastly, it's crucial to avoid overestimating how much you'll get from Social Security. Many people assume that Social Security benefits will cover most of their retirement expenses, but the reality is that it's only designed to replace about 40% of your pre-retirement income. Relying too heavily on this income stream can leave you short when it comes to covering living expenses in your golden years. That's why it's so important to supplement Social Security with your own savings and investments.

Recognizing Financial Traps and Learning to Steer Clear

Financial traps can come in many forms, but they all have one thing in common: they derail your retirement planning. Recognizing these traps early on—and learning how to steer clear of them—can save you from costly mistakes down the road.

One of the most common traps is falling for high-fee investments. Whether it's a mutual fund with hidden fees or a financial advisor charging high commissions, these costs can eat away at your returns over time. It might not seem like much at first glance, but over decades, even a small percentage can add up to thousands of dollars in lost gains. The key is to be diligent about understanding the fees associated with your investments and choosing low-cost options, like index funds, whenever possible.

Another trap to watch out for is lifestyle inflation. As you earn more throughout your career, it's natural to want to upgrade your lifestyle—nicer clothes, a bigger house, more vacations. But if you increase your spending every time your income goes up, you'll have less to save for retirement. It's important to find a balance between enjoying the fruits of your labor today and ensuring you have enough for tomorrow. One strategy is to commit to saving a percentage of every raise or bonus you receive, rather than letting lifestyle inflation creep in.

Debt is another major trap that can hinder your retirement savings. Whether it's credit card debt, student loans, or a mortgage, paying off debt takes away from the money you could be saving for retirement. While it's not always possible to avoid debt altogether, it's important to have a plan for paying it off as quickly and efficiently as possible. High-interest debt, like credit card balances, should be prioritized, as the interest charges can quickly spiral out of control and derail your financial goals.

Lastly, beware of investment scams. As people near retirement, they often become targets for fraudsters promising guaranteed high returns with little to no risk. The reality is that all investments come with some level of risk, and if something sounds too good to be true, it probably is. Stick to reputable financial institutions, do your research, and be wary of anyone pressuring you to make quick decisions about your money.

The Emotional Side of Retirement Planning: Keeping Stress Out

It's easy to think of retirement planning as purely a numbers game—how much you need to save, what investments to choose, when to start drawing on your benefits. But the emotional side of retirement planning is just as important, and it's something that often gets overlooked.

One of the biggest sources of stress in retirement planning is the fear of running out of money. This fear can lead people to either save obsessively, sacrificing their current quality of life, or to ignore the problem altogether, hoping it will somehow sort itself out. Neither approach is healthy. The key is to create a plan that balances saving for the future with living in the present. It's about finding peace of mind in knowing you're on the right track, rather than constantly worrying about whether you're doing enough.

Another emotional challenge is dealing with the uncertainty of the future. Retirement planning requires making a lot of assumptions—how long you'll live, what your health will be like, what the economy will do. This uncertainty can lead to anxiety and paralysis, making it difficult to make decisions. The best way to combat this is to focus on what you can control. While you can't predict the future, you can make educated guesses based on your current health, lifestyle, and financial situation. You can also build flexibility into your plan, so you have options if things don't go exactly as expected.

There's also the emotional challenge of transitioning from a mindset of saving to one of spending. For decades, you've been told to save, save, save, and when you finally retire, it can be hard to shift gears and start drawing on those savings. Some people feel guilty or anxious about spending their retirement funds, even though that's what they've been saving for all along. It's important to remind yourself that you've worked hard to build your nest egg, and it's okay to enjoy the fruits of your labor. Creating a detailed budget for retirement can help ease the transition by giving you a clear plan for how much you can spend each month without depleting your savings too quickly.

Lastly, retirement can bring up a lot of emotions around identity and purpose. For many people, their career is a big part of who they are, and leaving that behind can feel like losing a part of themselves. This can lead to feelings of loss, anxiety, or even depression. It's important to plan not just for the financial side of retirement, but for the emotional and social side as well. Think about how you'll spend your time, what hobbies or interests you want to pursue, and how you'll stay connected with friends and family. Having a sense of purpose in retirement can make a huge difference in your overall happiness and well-being.

MAXIMIZING YOUR INCOME STREAMS IN RETIREMENT

When you think about retirement, your mind might immediately jump to savings, but there's a lot more to it than that. In fact, maximizing your income streams in retirement is just as crucial as the savings you've built over time. This means making the most of what's already available to you—like Social Security—while also getting creative with alternative strategies for passive income. The ultimate goal is to create multiple sources of income that provide stability, flexibility, and the peace of mind that your golden years will be free from financial worry.

Social Security Demystified

Social Security is often the cornerstone of retirement planning, but there's a lot of confusion around how it works and how you can maximize it. The reality is that Social Security was never meant to be your sole source of income in retirement—it was designed to replace only a portion of your pre-retirement income. However, with careful planning, you can ensure that you're squeezing every possible benefit out of the system.

Let's start with the basics. Social Security benefits are based on your 35 highest-earning years. If you don't have 35 years of earnings, zeros are factored into the calculation, which can lower your benefit. This is why it's crucial to ensure you're working and earning as consistently as possible in those years leading up to retirement. Every additional year of work you put in can potentially replace a low-earning year or a zero, increasing your benefit.

Next, the age at which you start claiming Social Security has a big impact on how much you'll receive. You can begin taking benefits as early as age 62, but if you do, you'll receive a reduced amount—up to 30% less than what you'd get at your full retirement age (which is between 66 and 67, depending on when you were born). On the other hand, if you delay claiming benefits past your full retirement age, your monthly benefit will increase by 8% for each year you wait, up until age 70. So, if you're in good health and can afford to delay, waiting can significantly boost your lifetime benefit.

But Social Security isn't just about your own benefit. If you're married, divorced, or widowed, you may be entitled to spousal or survivor benefits, which can provide a substantial boost to your retirement income. For example, if your spouse earns more than you, you can claim up to 50% of their Social Security benefit, even if you never worked. If you're divorced and were married for at least 10 years, you can still claim spousal benefits based on your ex-spouse's earnings, as long as you haven't remarried. And if your spouse passes away, you may be eligible for survivor benefits, which could equal 100% of what they were receiving.

Social Security is complicated, but that complexity also presents opportunities to maximize your benefits if you know how to navigate the system. Consulting with a financial advisor who specializes in Social Security can help ensure that you're making the best possible decisions for your situation.

Passive Income and Alternative Strategies: Thinking Beyond the Obvious

While Social Security provides a reliable foundation, it's rarely enough to cover all of your retirement expenses. This is where passive income and alternative strategies come into play. When most people think of passive income, they imagine things like rental properties or dividends from stocks, but there are actually a wide variety of ways to generate income in retirement that don't require full-time work.

Rental income is a popular choice for many retirees because it can provide a steady stream of cash flow with relatively low effort, especially if you hire a property manager to handle day-to-day operations. If you already own a home, downsizing or renting out part of your property—like a basement apartment—can also be a way to generate extra income without having to take on the responsibility of managing an additional property.

Dividend-paying stocks are another common source of passive income. The beauty of dividend income is that it's typically taxed at a lower rate than ordinary income, and it allows you to benefit from the long-term growth of the stock market. However, it's important to diversify your investments and not rely too heavily on any one stock or sector. Look for companies with a long history of stable and increasing dividend payments, and consider investing in dividend-focused mutual funds or exchange-traded funds (ETFs) to further spread your risk.

For those willing to think outside the box, there are a number of alternative passive income strategies that can supplement your retirement income. Peer-to-peer lending platforms, for example, allow you to earn interest by lending money directly to individuals or small businesses. While these platforms carry more risk than traditional bank accounts, they can offer higher returns. Similarly, investing in real estate crowdfunding can give you exposure to the real estate market without the hassle of managing properties yourself.

Then there's the gig economy, which isn't exactly passive but can be a flexible way to generate income on your own terms. Platforms like Airbnb, Turo (for renting out your car), and various freelance marketplaces can allow you to leverage assets you already own or skills you've built over the years to bring in extra cash without committing to a traditional job. You can also consider creating digital products like e-books, online courses, or print-on-demand merchandise, which can generate sales with minimal ongoing effort once they're created.

Whatever passive income strategies you choose, it's important to have a plan for how that income will fit into your overall retirement budget. Make sure you're accounting for any taxes, fees, or maintenance costs associated with your passive income streams, and be realistic about how much effort they'll require. Passive income isn't always truly passive—there's usually some initial work involved—but the rewards can be well worth it.

Building Backup Plans - Safety Nets that Work

Even the best-laid retirement plans can go awry. Whether it's an unexpected health issue, a downturn in the stock market, or a sudden increase in living expenses, life has a way of throwing curveballs. That's why it's so important to have backup plans in place to protect your financial security.

One of the most effective safety nets is a robust emergency fund. Even in retirement, it's important to have enough cash set aside to cover at least three to six months' worth of living expenses. This fund should be kept in a liquid, easily accessible account like a high-yield savings account, rather than tied up in investments that could fluctuate in value. Having an emergency fund can help you avoid dipping into your retirement savings—or worse, going into debt—when the unexpected happens.

Another key safety net is long-term care insurance. As you age, the likelihood of needing some form of long-term care—whether it's in-home care, assisted living, or a nursing home—increases. Unfortunately, Medicare doesn't cover most long-term care services, and the costs can be staggering. Long-term care insurance can help cover these expenses, allowing you to preserve your savings and avoid becoming a financial burden on your family. The earlier you purchase long-term care insurance, the lower your premiums will be, so it's worth considering this option well before you need it.

If you own a home, your home equity can also serve as a backup plan. A reverse mortgage, for example, allows you to tap into your home's equity without having to sell it. While reverse mortgages have their drawbacks—such as fees and interest that can add up over time—they can be a viable option for retirees who are house-rich but cash-poor. Another option is downsizing to a smaller, more affordable home, which can free up cash and reduce your living expenses.

Annuities are another tool that can provide a steady stream of income in retirement. Unlike traditional investments, which fluctuate with the market, annuities offer guaranteed payments for a set period of time, or even for life. This can provide peace of mind, knowing that you'll have a consistent income no matter what happens to your other investments. However, annuities can be complex and often come with high fees, so it's important to fully understand the terms before committing.

Lastly, don't overlook the importance of having a solid estate plan. While it might not directly impact your retirement income, an estate plan ensures that your assets are distributed according to your wishes and that your loved ones are taken care of. This includes having a will, a living trust (if necessary), and powers of attorney for healthcare and finances. Having these documents in place can save your family from unnecessary stress and legal battles, and it can give you peace of mind knowing that your affairs are in order.

By building these backup plans into your retirement strategy, you'll be better prepared to weather whatever challenges come your way. Whether it's an unexpected expense, a market downturn, or a health issue, having safety nets in place ensures that you can enjoy your retirement with confidence, knowing that you've covered all your bases.

THE TIME FACTOR

When should you retire?

When it comes to retirement, timing can be everything. Deciding when to retire is one of the most personal and impactful financial decisions you'll ever make. It's not just about the money, though finances are a big part of the equation. It's also about lifestyle, health, personal goals, and even unexpected life events that can force your hand. Whether you're dreaming of retiring early, working a bit longer for a bigger nest egg, or just trying to figure out the best moment to hang up your hat, understanding the time factor in retirement is crucial. Let's dive into how the timing of your retirement can shape the rest of your life.

Early Retirement vs. Delayed Retirement: Pros, Cons, and Surprises

Retiring early sounds like a dream. Who wouldn't want more time to travel, relax, or spend with family? But like most things, early retirement comes with trade-offs, and it's not all sunshine and beaches. On the flip side, delaying retirement might not be as glamorous, but it can offer some serious financial perks that pay off in the long run. Understanding the pros, cons, and some of the surprises along the way can help you decide whether to retire early or stay in the workforce a little longer.

One of the biggest perks of early retirement is the freedom to enjoy life on your terms sooner rather than later. Whether that means exploring new hobbies, volunteering, or traveling the world, retiring early gives you the gift of time. But this freedom comes with a cost: your retirement savings will need to stretch over a longer period. Retiring early means fewer years to save and more years to withdraw from your savings. If you stop working in your 50s, for example, you could be looking at 30 or even 40 years of retirement, which means you need a significant nest egg to avoid outliving your money.

There's also the issue of healthcare. In the U.S., Medicare doesn't kick in until age 65, so if you retire before then, you'll need to find another way to cover healthcare costs. Private insurance can be expensive, and if you have any health issues, those costs can escalate quickly. Some retirees bridge the gap with employer-sponsored retiree health insurance, but not all employers offer that benefit.

On the other hand, delaying retirement allows you to build up a bigger retirement fund and take advantage of the increased benefits that come with waiting. For example, your Social Security benefits increase by about 8% for each year you delay claiming them past your full retirement age (up until age 70). This can make a huge difference in your monthly income later in life. Additionally, working longer allows your investments more time to grow and accumulate interest, meaning you'll have a larger cushion when you eventually do retire.

But there are surprises on both sides of the equation. Some early retirees find that they miss the structure and social interaction of work, or that they get bored with all that free time. Others encounter financial setbacks like a market downturn or unexpected expenses that force them to go back to work. On the flip side, those who delay retirement often find they have more energy and motivation than they expected, enjoying their work well into their 60s or even 70s.

Ultimately, the decision between early retirement and delayed retirement comes down to your personal goals, financial situation, and health. There's no one-size-fits-all answer, but weighing the pros and cons can help you make an informed decision.

The Age Factor: How Timing Affects Your Savings

The age at which you retire has a profound effect on how much you need to save and how long your savings will last. It's not just about picking a date on the calendar—it's about understanding how different retirement ages impact your financial future.

Let's start with the basics. The earlier you retire, the more you'll need to have saved, simply because your savings need to last longer. If you retire at 62, for example, you might need to support yourself for 25 to 30 years, depending on your life expectancy. That means your retirement savings need to be substantial enough to cover not just day-to-day expenses but also healthcare, unexpected costs, and inflation.

One of the most significant financial benefits of working longer is the potential to supercharge your retirement savings. The last few years of your working life are often when you're earning the most, meaning you can make larger contributions to your 401(k) or IRA. In fact, starting at age 50, you can take advantage of catch-up contributions, which allow you to put more money into your retirement accounts than younger workers. This can make a big difference in your overall savings.

Additionally, the longer you work, the more you can take advantage of the power of compound interest. This is especially important if you've invested in the stock market or other growth-oriented investments. Every extra year your money stays invested means more growth, and over time, that growth compounds, giving you a bigger nest egg when you finally do retire.

Then there's Social Security. As mentioned earlier, the age at which you start claiming Social Security benefits can significantly impact how much you receive. If you claim benefits as soon as you're eligible at age 62, your monthly check will be reduced by up to 30% compared to what you'd get if you waited until your full retirement age (between 66 and 67). If you hold off even longer, until age 70, you'll get an 8% boost for each year you delay. This can add up to a much larger monthly benefit over the course of your retirement.

But there's more to consider than just the numbers. Your health and lifestyle play a big role in determining when to retire. If you're in good health and enjoy your job, working longer can be a smart financial move. But if you're dealing with health issues or simply don't enjoy your work anymore, retiring earlier might be worth the trade-off of a smaller savings cushion.

In the end, the age factor is about balance. Retiring too early without enough savings can leave you struggling later in life, but working too long can rob you of the opportunity to enjoy your retirement while you're still healthy and active. The key is to find the sweet spot that works for you, based on your financial goals, health, and personal priorities.

What to Do When Life Throws a Curveball

No matter how carefully you plan, life has a way of throwing unexpected challenges your way. Whether it's a health crisis, a family emergency, or an economic downturn, life's curveballs can derail even the best-laid retirement plans. The key is to stay flexible and have a backup plan in place so you're not caught off guard.

One of the most common curveballs people face as they approach retirement is a sudden job loss. Whether it's due to layoffs, company restructuring, or health issues that force you out of the workforce earlier than expected, losing your job close to retirement can be a major financial blow. If this happens to you, the first step is to take a deep breath and reassess your financial situation. Look at your savings, your expenses, and your potential sources of income—such as unemployment benefits or part-time work—and come up with a plan to get you through the transition.

If you're still several years away from your planned retirement age, you may need to tighten your budget and focus on building up your emergency fund. You might also consider looking for part-time or freelance work to bring in some extra income while you search for a full-time job. And if you're close to retirement, it might be time to start thinking about whether you can retire a little earlier than planned, or if you need to dip into your savings to cover the gap.

Another common curveball is an unexpected health issue. Healthcare costs can be one of the biggest expenses in retirement, especially if you retire before age 65 and don't yet qualify for Medicare. If you're hit with a health crisis, it's important to have a plan for how you'll cover medical expenses. This might mean tapping into your health savings account (HSA) if you have one, or looking into options like COBRA or private health insurance to bridge the gap until Medicare kicks in.

For many retirees, the stock market itself can be a curveball. A major market downturn right before or during retirement can significantly reduce the value of your investments, leaving you with less money to live on. If this happens, it's important to stay calm and avoid making rash decisions. Selling off investments during a downturn can lock in your losses, so it's often better to ride out the storm if you can. This is where having a diversified portfolio can really pay off. If you've spread your investments across different asset classes—such as stocks, bonds, and real estate—you'll be better positioned to weather market volatility.

Finally, family emergencies can also throw a wrench into your retirement plans. Whether it's helping out a grown child who's struggling financially or caring for an aging parent, family responsibilities can sometimes require you to dip into your savings earlier than expected. While it's natural to want to help loved ones, it's important to balance their needs with your own financial security. If possible, try to set boundaries or explore other options—such as government assistance programs for elderly parents—before depleting your retirement funds.

When life throws a curveball, the most important thing is to stay flexible and adaptable. Having an emergency fund, keeping your skills sharp, and staying open to part-time or freelance work can all help you navigate the unexpected and stay on track toward your retirement goals.

ADJUSTING FOR THE UNKNOWN

When planning for retirement, we often focus on what we can predict—our savings, our Social Security benefits, and maybe even how we want to spend our time. But life is unpredictable, and the unknowns can be the biggest challenge when it comes to your financial security in retirement. Whether it's rising healthcare costs, inflation, or unexpected life events, learning how to adjust for these variables is key to building a retirement plan that can withstand the test of time. The good news? You can prepare for these unknowns with confidence, ensuring that your retirement remains financially stable and enjoyable.

Preparing for Healthcare Costs: Reality, Not Scare Tactics

One of the most common fears about retirement is how to manage healthcare costs. It's no secret that healthcare expenses tend to increase as we age, but there's a lot of confusion and, frankly, fear-mongering around how much you really need to save for medical bills. Preparing for healthcare costs in retirement is essential, but it's important to separate reality from scare tactics.

First, let's look at the facts. Yes, healthcare can be expensive. A study by Fidelity Investments estimates that the average 65-year-old couple retiring in 2023 will need about $315,000 to cover medical expenses throughout retirement. That number can feel daunting, but it's important to remember that this figure includes everything from Medicare premiums to out-of-pocket costs like co-pays, prescription drugs, and long-term care. It's also spread out over 20 to 30 years, not required all at once.

Medicare, which kicks in at age 65, will cover a large portion of your medical expenses, but it's not free, and it doesn't cover everything. You'll still need to budget for premiums, deductibles, and co-payments, as well as services like dental, vision, and hearing care, which aren't covered by Medicare. If you retire before age 65, you'll also need to account for health insurance to cover the gap until you're eligible for Medicare, which can be a significant expense.

One way to prepare for healthcare costs is by opening a Health Savings Account (HSA) if you're eligible. An HSA is a tax-advantaged account that allows you to save money specifically for medical expenses. The best part? HSA contributions are tax-deductible, the money grows tax-free, and withdrawals for qualified medical expenses are also tax-free. Even if you don't end up using all the money in your HSA, it can be used for non-medical expenses after age 65, though you'll pay regular income tax on those withdrawals.

Another way to manage healthcare costs in retirement is by considering supplemental insurance, often called Medigap. These policies can help cover some of the costs that Medicare doesn't, like deductibles and co-payments. While Medigap plans have monthly premiums, they can provide peace of mind by reducing your out-of-pocket expenses.

The key to preparing for healthcare costs is planning for them, but not letting them overwhelm you. By understanding your Medicare options, considering supplemental insurance, and saving in an HSA if possible, you can manage these expenses without letting fear dictate your retirement plans.

Inflation-Proofing Your Retirement

Inflation is one of those sneaky forces that can quietly erode your purchasing power over time. Even a relatively low inflation rate of 2% to 3% can have a significant impact on your retirement savings over 20 or 30 years. That's why it's essential to inflation-proof your retirement to ensure that your money stretches as far as you need it to.

The first step to protecting yourself against inflation is understanding how it works. Inflation refers to the general rise in prices over time. This means that the same amount of money will buy less in the future than it does today. For example, if inflation averages 3% per year, something that costs $1,000 today will cost over $1,800 in 20 years. If you're living on a fixed income in retirement, this can be a real problem.

One of the best ways to guard against inflation is to make sure your investments are positioned for growth. While conservative investments like bonds can provide stability, they typically don't keep pace with inflation. Stocks, on the other hand, have historically outperformed inflation over the long term. While stocks come with more risk, having a diversified portfolio that includes some exposure to equities can help your retirement savings grow and keep pace with rising prices.

Another tool for inflation-proofing your retirement is Treasury Inflation-Protected Securities (TIPS). TIPS are government bonds that are specifically designed to protect against inflation. The principal value of TIPS increases with inflation, as measured by the Consumer Price Index (CPI). This means that when inflation rises, so does the value of your TIPS investment. While the returns on TIPS may not be as high as stocks, they provide a guaranteed hedge against inflation.

Social Security also plays a role in inflation-proofing your retirement. Social Security benefits are adjusted for inflation each year through a cost-of-living adjustment (COLA). While the COLA doesn't always fully match the true rise in living costs, it does provide some protection against inflation for retirees. The longer you delay claiming Social Security, the larger your monthly benefit will be, and the COLA will apply to that higher benefit for the rest of your life.

In addition to your investments and Social Security, your lifestyle choices can also help protect against inflation. If you plan to downsize your home or move to a lower-cost area in retirement, you may be able to offset some of the effects of inflation by reducing your living expenses. Similarly, maintaining a flexible budget that allows for adjustments as prices rise can help you stay ahead of inflation without sacrificing your quality of life.

Inflation is a reality of life, but it doesn't have to derail your retirement plans. By investing for growth, considering inflation-protected investments, and making smart lifestyle choices, you can ensure that your savings keep up with rising costs.

Handling Unexpected Life Events with Confidence

No matter how carefully you plan, life has a way of throwing unexpected challenges your way. Whether it's a health crisis, a family emergency, or an economic downturn, handling these curveballs with confidence is key to maintaining your financial security in retirement.

The first step in preparing for the unexpected is building a solid emergency fund. Ideally, you should have enough cash set aside to cover at least six months of living expenses. This will give you a financial cushion to fall back on if something unexpected happens, like a medical emergency or a major home repair. An emergency fund can help you avoid dipping into your retirement savings or selling investments during a market downturn, which could hurt your long-term financial security.

In addition to an emergency fund, having the right insurance in place is crucial for handling life's curveballs. Long-term care insurance, for example, can help cover the cost of a nursing home or in-home care if you need it. This type of care can be incredibly expensive, and without insurance, it can quickly drain your retirement savings. Long-term care insurance can give you peace of mind knowing that you're covered if you ever need assistance with daily living activities.

Another form of insurance to consider is life insurance, particularly if you have dependents or a spouse who would be financially impacted by your passing. While life insurance is typically more important earlier in life when you have young children or a mortgage, it can still play a role in retirement planning, especially if you want to leave a financial legacy or ensure your spouse is taken care of.

Estate planning is another important aspect of preparing for the unknown. Having a will, a healthcare directive, and a power of attorney in place can ensure that your wishes are carried out if something happens to you. It can also make things easier for your loved ones, reducing the financial and emotional burden during an already difficult time.

Finally, staying flexible and adaptable is key to handling life's surprises. Retirement is a long journey, and things will inevitably change along the way. Whether it's a market downturn that affects your investments or a family emergency that requires your attention, being willing to adjust your plans and make changes as needed will help you navigate the unknown with confidence.

Handling unexpected life events doesn't mean you need to have all the answers ahead of time. It's about building a strong financial foundation, having the right insurance and legal documents in place, and staying flexible enough to adapt to whatever comes your way. With these steps in place, you can approach retirement with confidence, knowing that you're prepared for the unknown.

MAKING YOUR MONEY LAST

The Exit Strategy

Retirement isn't just about reaching a certain age and stepping away from work; it's also about ensuring that the money you've worked so hard to save can last throughout the remainder of your life. Crafting an exit strategy for your finances is essential if you want to maintain a comfortable lifestyle without the fear of running out of money. It's like planning a long road trip—you know where you want to go, but you need to make sure you have enough fuel in the tank to get there. In this case, that fuel is your retirement savings, and making it last requires a blend of careful planning, thoughtful spending, and smart investment choices.

How to Spend Wisely Without Sacrificing Comfort

When you retire, managing your spending becomes one of the most important aspects of ensuring that your money will last. While the temptation may be to splurge—after all, you've earned it—overspending in the early years of retirement can quickly deplete your savings. However, spending wisely doesn't mean living a life of deprivation or giving up the things that bring you joy. It's about striking a balance between enjoying your retirement and making sure that you don't outlive your savings.

One of the best ways to approach spending in retirement is to create a budget that reflects your priorities. Start by separating your essential expenses, such as housing, healthcare, food, and utilities, from your discretionary expenses, like travel, dining out, and hobbies. This will give you a clear picture of how much of your income is going toward necessities and how much is available for the fun stuff. From there, you can make adjustments to ensure that your spending aligns with your financial goals.

For many retirees, housing is one of the biggest expenses. Downsizing to a smaller home, moving to a less expensive area, or even exploring options like senior living communities can reduce your monthly costs and free up money for other activities. It's also worth considering how much of your discretionary spending you want to devote to travel or other experiences in the early years of retirement, when you're likely to have the most energy and mobility. By planning ahead, you can avoid spending too much too soon, allowing you to maintain a comfortable lifestyle throughout your retirement years.

One trick to managing spending without feeling restricted is the 50/30/20 rule. This simple framework divides your income into three categories: 50% for needs, 30% for wants, and 20% for savings or debt repayment. While it's often used by younger individuals, this rule can also be applied in retirement to keep your spending in check while still allowing room for enjoyment. Remember, it's not about denying yourself the pleasures of life, but rather about making intentional choices that ensure your financial security for years to come.

Lastly, stay aware of lifestyle inflation. It's easy to get caught up in the mindset of "I deserve this," especially after working hard for so many years, but keeping an eye on how small luxuries add up can make a big difference. Occasional treats are fine, but routine indulgence can chip away at your savings. Being mindful of your spending patterns can help keep your finances on track without sacrificing the comfort you deserve.

Withdrawal Strategies: Stretching Your Savings the Right Way

Once you retire, figuring out how to withdraw from your savings is just as crucial as deciding how much to save in the first place. The goal is to stretch your nest egg for as long as possible, and doing so requires a withdrawal strategy that balances income generation with preserving your principal.

One of the most well-known approaches is the 4% rule. This rule suggests that you can safely withdraw 4% of your savings in the first year of retirement and then adjust that amount each year for inflation. For example, if you retire with $1 million saved, you would withdraw $40,000 in the first year. The idea is that by withdrawing this amount, you'll avoid depleting your savings too quickly while still giving yourself enough income to live on.

While the 4% rule can be a helpful guideline, it's not foolproof. It assumes a steady rate of return on your investments and doesn't account for market volatility or personal spending habits. If you experience significant market downturns in the early years of retirement or have large, unexpected expenses, withdrawing 4% may not be sustainable. In these cases, it might make sense to be more flexible with your withdrawal rate, adjusting it based on your portfolio's performance and your current needs.

Another popular strategy is the bucket approach, which divides your savings into different "buckets" based on when you'll need the money. For example, you might have a short-term bucket for the first five years of retirement, filled with more conservative investments like bonds or cash, and a long-term bucket for years 10 and beyond, invested more aggressively in stocks. The idea is to draw from the short-term bucket first, giving your long-term investments time to grow. As you move through retirement, you periodically refill the short-term bucket from the long-term bucket. This method helps protect against market fluctuations and ensures that you always have money available when you need it.

Additionally, it's important to consider the order in which you withdraw from different accounts. Traditional wisdom says to start by withdrawing from taxable accounts, followed by tax-deferred accounts like traditional IRAs or 401(k)s, and finally from tax-free accounts like Roth IRAs. This strategy can help minimize your tax liability in retirement and allow your tax-advantaged accounts to continue growing tax-free for as long as possible.

Keep in mind that mandatory withdrawals, known as Required Minimum Distributions (RMDs), kick in at age 73 (as of 2023) for most retirement accounts, including traditional IRAs and 401(k)s. These withdrawals are required by law and are based on your life expectancy and the account balance. Failing to take your RMDs can result in hefty penalties, so make sure you plan for these withdrawals as part of your overall strategy.

Ultimately, the key to stretching your savings is flexibility. No one can predict the future with certainty, so having a plan that allows for adjustments along the way will give you the best chance of making your money last for the duration of your retirement.

Protecting Your Nest Egg: Simple Steps for Longevity

While crafting a withdrawal strategy is important, protecting your nest egg from potential threats is equally critical. From market downturns to unexpected expenses, there are several factors that could erode your savings if you're not prepared. The good news is that there are simple steps you can take to safeguard your financial future and ensure that your money lasts as long as you need it to.

One of the best ways to protect your nest egg is by maintaining a diversified investment portfolio. Diversification involves spreading your investments across different asset classes—such as stocks, bonds, and real estate—so that no single investment dominates your portfolio. This helps reduce your overall risk, as the poor performance of one asset class can be offset by gains in another. While diversification doesn't guarantee against losses, it can provide a level of protection against market volatility, helping to preserve your savings over the long term.

Another critical step in protecting your nest egg is having an emergency fund. Even in retirement, unexpected expenses will pop up—whether it's a major home repair, a medical emergency, or a family member in need of financial help. Without an emergency fund, you may be forced to withdraw from your retirement savings at an inopportune time, which can have a lasting impact on your portfolio. Ideally, your emergency fund should cover at least six months of living expenses and be held in a liquid, easily accessible account.

In addition to an emergency fund, having the right insurance can also help protect your savings. Long-term care insurance, for example, can cover the cost of assisted living or in-home care, which can be financially devastating if not planned for. While long-term care insurance can be expensive, it's often worth the peace of mind knowing that you won't have to drain your savings to pay for care if the need arises.

It's also important to consider the impact of inflation on your retirement savings. Even modest inflation can erode your purchasing power over time, especially if you're living on a fixed income. To protect against this, make sure that a portion of your portfolio is invested in assets that have the potential to outpace inflation, such as stocks or inflation-protected bonds (like Treasury Inflation-Protected Securities, or TIPS). Keeping your investments aligned with inflation will help ensure that your savings maintain their value over time.

Another simple yet effective way to protect your nest egg is by avoiding unnecessary fees and taxes. This means being mindful of the fees associated with your investments, such as mutual fund expense ratios or trading commissions, and choosing low-cost options whenever possible. It also means taking advantage of tax-advantaged accounts like Roth IRAs, which allow your savings to grow tax-free and can provide a valuable source of tax-free income in retirement.

Lastly, don't underestimate the importance of reviewing your plan regularly. Just as your needs and goals change over time, so should your retirement strategy. Life events like a change in health, a new grandchild, or even an inheritance can all impact your financial plan. By reviewing your plan at least once a year and making adjustments as needed, you can stay on track to protect your nest egg and ensure that your money lasts throughout your retirement.

Protecting your savings isn't about making drastic changes or taking on unnecessary risks. It's about making smart, thoughtful decisions that safeguard your financial future. By diversifying your investments, maintaining an emergency fund, and staying vigilant about fees and taxes, you can enjoy the retirement you've always dreamed of—without worrying about outliving your money.

LIVING YOUR BEST LIFE AFTER RETIREMENT

Retirement is often seen as the final chapter in the book of life, but in reality, it's just the beginning of a new adventure. This stage of life presents an opportunity to pursue passions, reinvent yourself, and finally focus on the things that bring you the most joy. However, as exciting as this new chapter can be, one of the biggest concerns is always money. How do you live the life of your dreams without the stress of financial strain looming over you? And once you've achieved financial security, how do you thrive mentally, emotionally, and socially? Let's dive into how you can create a lifestyle you'll love and truly live your best life after retirement.

How to Create a Lifestyle You'll Love Without Stressing About Money

One of the most liberating aspects of retirement is having the freedom to create your own lifestyle. No more alarm clocks dictating your day, no more office stress, and no more juggling work-life balance. But with this newfound freedom can come a very real fear—running out of money. The good news is that with careful planning and some smart financial habits, you can build a life that's both fulfilling and financially sustainable.

First, it's essential to redefine what "living well" means to you. Many people equate a high-quality lifestyle with spending lots of money—whether it's on expensive vacations, luxurious homes, or lavish entertainment. But after retirement, it's time to rethink what truly makes you happy. Ask yourself, "What do I really need to feel fulfilled?" You might find that it's not about material wealth at all. For many retirees, it's the simple joys—spending time with loved ones, pursuing hobbies, volunteering, or traveling more slowly and deeply—that create a rich and rewarding life.

A key element in managing your money well during retirement is understanding your cash flow. This is where having a realistic and well-thought-out budget becomes critical. Start by calculating your fixed expenses, such as housing, healthcare, utilities, and groceries. Once you know how much you need to cover the basics, you can then allocate funds toward discretionary expenses—like hobbies, dining out, or travel. Make sure your spending aligns with your core values and what you enjoy most. Remember, it's not about cutting out all the fun; it's about prioritizing what truly brings you happiness and cutting out wasteful or unnecessary spending.

Another way to reduce financial stress is to downsize where necessary. Perhaps your home is larger than you need now that the kids are grown and gone. Downsizing can free up equity, reduce maintenance costs, and lower utility bills. Many retirees find that moving to a smaller, more manageable home is not only financially beneficial but also emotionally freeing.

Additionally, consider creating multiple streams of income during retirement. While Social Security and your retirement savings may form the core of your income, having side income from part-time work, rental properties, or even a hobby-turned-business can provide an extra layer of financial security. This not only reduces the stress of relying on a fixed income but can also keep you engaged and productive during your retirement years.

Finally, don't underestimate the power of mindful spending. Rather than focusing on acquiring more things, shift your mindset to valuing experiences and meaningful connections. Research shows that spending money on experiences, like traveling or learning new skills, tends to bring more lasting happiness than spending on material goods. When you spend money, do so with intention—this will help you get the most joy out of your dollars without feeling like you're sacrificing your financial future.

Thriving in Retirement: Beyond Just Financial Security

While financial security is a critical aspect of retirement, thriving during these years goes far beyond just having enough money in the bank. It's about staying mentally and physically active, building strong relationships, and nurturing a sense of purpose. After all, what's the point of having a well-padded retirement account if you're not emotionally fulfilled or physically healthy enough to enjoy it?

One of the best ways to thrive in retirement is by staying physically active. Exercise not only boosts your physical health but also improves your mental well-being. Regular physical activity can reduce the risk of chronic diseases, improve mobility, and even enhance your mood by releasing endorphins—your body's natural feel-good chemicals. Whether you enjoy walking, swimming, yoga, or joining a local fitness class, staying active will help you maintain your vitality and energy well into your retirement years.

Social connections are equally important. Loneliness and isolation are real risks in retirement, especially if you're no longer in regular contact with colleagues or if your social circle has shrunk over the years. That's why it's essential to make an effort to build and maintain relationships. Whether it's with family, old friends, or new acquaintances, having a strong support system can significantly impact your emotional well-being. Consider joining clubs, attending community events, or volunteering—anything that keeps you connected and engaged with others. Many retirees also find fulfillment in mentorship, passing down their knowledge and experience to younger generations.

In addition to staying active and socially connected, one of the most important elements of thriving in retirement is finding a sense of purpose. For years, your identity may have been closely tied to your career, but now that you're retired, it's time to redefine what gives your life meaning. For some, this might mean pursuing hobbies or learning new skills—perhaps you've always wanted to paint, play an instrument, or write a book. Others find purpose in giving back to their communities through volunteering or charitable work. Whatever it is, having something to wake up for each day will give you a sense of fulfillment and direction.

Moreover, retirement is an ideal time to prioritize personal growth. This might involve traveling to new places, expanding your knowledge, or even taking time to reflect on the life you've built and the legacy you want to leave behind. Consider developing a practice of mindfulness or meditation to help you stay present and appreciate the richness of this phase of life.

Ultimately, thriving in retirement is about balancing the practicalities of financial security with the pursuit of mental, physical, and emotional well-being. It's about embracing the freedom to live on your own terms while maintaining a sense of purpose and joy in your daily life.

Retirement Isn't the End, It's the Next Adventure

For many people, retirement represents the end of a long career and the closing of one chapter of life. But in truth, retirement is the start of an entirely new adventure—one filled with opportunities for exploration, discovery, and growth. The key is to approach this stage with an open mind and a sense of curiosity.

Think of retirement as a blank slate. Without the demands of a full-time job, you finally have the time to explore the world in ways you never could before. Maybe you've always dreamed of traveling the world—now's your chance to do it. Whether it's visiting new countries, exploring different cultures, or simply taking a road trip to see parts of your own country, travel can be one of the most enriching experiences of retirement.

And you don't need to break the bank to do it. Traveling slowly, staying in budget accommodations, or taking advantage of senior discounts can help you see the world without straining your finances.

For those who prefer a quieter pace of life, retirement can be a time to dive into new hobbies or deepen your skills in areas you already love. From gardening to woodworking to learning a new language, retirement offers endless possibilities for personal growth. Many retirees also find great satisfaction in continuing to contribute to society in some capacity, whether through volunteering, mentoring, or even part-time work in a new field.

Importantly, the mindset you bring to retirement will shape your experience of it. Viewing this phase of life as an adventure opens up possibilities you might not have considered before. Maybe you've always been curious about a particular subject—now you can take a course at your local college or online. Perhaps you've always wanted to try something completely out of your comfort zone, like skydiving or painting. The beauty of retirement is that you have the freedom to explore these interests without the pressures of a traditional 9-to-5 job.

Additionally, don't shy away from challenging yourself during retirement. While it's tempting to slow down and take it easy, continuing to set goals for yourself—whether they're physical, intellectual, or emotional—will keep you sharp and engaged with life. Retirement can be a time to reinvent yourself, whether that means switching to a new career or finally pursuing that passion project you've always put off.

And remember, just because you're retired doesn't mean you have to stop contributing to society. Many retirees find fulfillment in staying active in their communities, whether through volunteer work, activism, or mentorship. There's a wealth of knowledge and experience that comes with age, and sharing that wisdom with others can be incredibly rewarding.

Ultimately, retirement isn't the end of the road—it's a new beginning, a chance to embark on the next big adventure of your life. It's a time to prioritize what truly matters, invest in relationships, pursue passions, and discover the joys that come from living on your own terms. Whether you choose to travel the world, dive into new hobbies, or continue making a difference in your community, the adventure of retirement is yours to shape. Embrace it fully, and make these years the most exciting and fulfilling chapter of your life yet.

YOUR PERSONALIZED ACTION PLAN

Ready, Set, Retire

Retirement can seem like a distant dream for many, but in reality, it's something that sneaks up on us faster than we expect. With so much to plan for—financial security, lifestyle choices, healthcare—it's no wonder people often feel overwhelmed when trying to map out their future. But here's the thing: it doesn't have to be overwhelming. The key to a smooth and confident transition into retirement is to break it down into simple, manageable steps, creating an action plan that fits your unique life and goals. With the right checklist, you can ensure you're on track, financially and emotionally, to fully enjoy the next phase of your life. Let's start building your personalized retirement action plan.

A Step-by-Step Checklist to Get Started Right Away

The first step to a successful retirement is making sure all the critical boxes are checked. The following checklist will help guide you through every essential aspect of retirement planning, so you can get started right away:

☐ **Set Your Retirement Goals**
Define what retirement means to you. Do you want to travel, start a hobby, or downsize? Establish what you hope to achieve in your golden years, and use these goals to shape the rest of your planning.

☐ **Calculate Your Retirement Needs**
Figure out how much income you'll need annually in retirement. Consider all your living expenses, including housing, healthcare, food, transportation, and leisure activities. Don't forget to account for inflation and unexpected costs.

☐ **Assess Your Current Financial Situation**
Take stock of all your assets—your savings, retirement accounts, investments, and other financial resources. Compare this to your retirement needs to identify any gaps.

☐ **Maximize Your Retirement Accounts**
Ensure you're contributing enough to your retirement accounts (401(k), IRA, or other pension plans). Take advantage of employer matching programs and make catch-up contributions if you're over 50.

☐ **Eliminate Debt**
If possible, enter retirement with little or no debt. Pay down high-interest debt like credit cards, and consider paying off your mortgage to reduce monthly expenses.

☐ **Create a Retirement Budget**
A detailed budget will give you a clear picture of how much you'll be spending versus what income you'll have in retirement. Plan for both fixed and discretionary expenses, making sure there's enough flexibility for unforeseen costs.

☐ **Plan for Healthcare Expenses**

Research your healthcare options. Medicare doesn't cover everything, so you'll want to explore supplemental insurance or long-term care insurance to fill in any gaps.

☐ **Build an Emergency Fund**

Even in retirement, life can throw curveballs. Set aside at least six months' worth of living expenses in a liquid savings account to cover emergencies without tapping into your retirement investments.

☐ **Determine Your Social Security Strategy**

Decide the best time to start claiming Social Security. Remember that waiting until your full retirement age or later will maximize your benefits.

☐ **Diversify Your Income Sources**

In addition to Social Security and retirement savings, look for other ways to generate income, such as rental properties, part-time work, or passive income streams.

☐ **Prepare Legal Documents**

Make sure your legal documents are up to date. This includes your will, power of attorney, healthcare proxy, and any trusts. These documents ensure that your wishes are carried out in case you're unable to make decisions for yourself.

☐ **Review Your Estate Plan**

Work with an estate planner to ensure your assets are distributed according to your wishes. This will help minimize taxes and prevent family disputes down the road.

☐ **Set a Retirement Date**

Once you've completed the previous steps, it's time to choose your retirement date. This can be flexible, but having a target will help you stay focused on your plan.

☐ **Create a Post-Retirement Plan**

What will you do with your time? Retirement is more than just stopping work—it's about having a fulfilling life. Think about your passions and how you'll structure your days.

This checklist provides a solid foundation for your retirement action plan. But don't worry if you need to tweak or adjust it along the way; the key is to have a starting point and move forward with confidence.

Sticking to the Plan (And What to Do When You Need to Adjust)

Creating a plan is one thing; sticking to it is a whole different story. Life, as we all know, doesn't always go according to plan. Retirement might come sooner than expected due to job changes, health issues, or other unforeseen circumstances. Or perhaps your savings don't grow as quickly as you'd hoped, and you need to adjust your strategy. That's okay! What matters is having the flexibility to adapt your plan while staying focused on your long-term goals.

First, recognize that adjustments are normal. The key to a successful retirement plan is its ability to be fluid. Think of it as a living, breathing document that changes as you do. The initial plan you create in your 40s or 50s may not look the same as the one you'll follow once you're 65 or older, and that's completely normal. Life happens, and so do adjustments.

When you find yourself needing to tweak the plan, the first step is to reassess your situation. Have your goals changed? Maybe your desire to travel has waned, and now you want to stay close to family. Or perhaps the cost of healthcare has increased more than you anticipated, and you need to allocate more funds to that area. Whatever the change, take time to sit down and re-evaluate your financial goals and lifestyle desires.

Once you've identified where adjustments are needed, revisit your budget. Budgeting during retirement is crucial because your income will likely be more fixed than it was during your working years. Regularly review your expenses and income to ensure that you're not overspending or depleting your savings too quickly. If you find that your current spending is unsustainable, don't panic. Start by trimming discretionary expenses, like dining out or luxury purchases, before making any drastic changes to your lifestyle.

Another area that might require adjustment is your investment strategy. When you're younger, you have more time to ride out the ups and downs of the stock market, but as you approach retirement, your investment strategy should become more conservative. That doesn't mean you should avoid risk entirely, but it's essential to strike a balance between growth and protection. If you're unsure of where to adjust, consider speaking with a financial advisor who can guide you based on your specific circumstances.

Finally, don't forget the emotional side of adjusting your retirement plan. Change can be difficult, especially when it involves your financial security. If you're feeling stressed or anxious about needing to make adjustments, take a step back and focus on the bigger picture. Remember that even if you have to make cuts or delays, you're still working toward a secure and fulfilling retirement. Keep your long-term goals in mind, and stay flexible enough to adapt as needed.

Building Confidence in Your Financial Future

Confidence in retirement planning doesn't come from having the perfect plan or an oversized bank account—it comes from knowing that you've done the necessary work to build a solid financial foundation. It's about trusting that, even when life throws you curveballs, you have the knowledge, resources, and flexibility to navigate the challenges and stay on course.

One of the most effective ways to build this confidence is by becoming financially literate. The more you know about personal finance, investments, and retirement planning, the better equipped you'll be to make informed decisions. Don't worry—you don't have to become an expert overnight. Start with the basics: understand how compound interest works, learn about different types of retirement accounts, and familiarize yourself with tax strategies. By gradually increasing your financial knowledge, you'll feel more in control of your future.

Another crucial element in building confidence is consistency. Planning for retirement isn't a one-time event; it's an ongoing process. Regularly review your financial situation, check in on your investments, and update your budget as needed. This will help you spot potential problems early on, giving you the chance to course-correct before things spiral out of control. Just as importantly, seeing your progress over time—whether it's in the form of growing savings or paying off debt—will give you a sense of accomplishment and confidence in your ability to achieve your goals.

It's also important to have a solid support system in place. This might include a financial advisor who can provide expert guidance, but it could also be friends or family members who have successfully navigated their own retirement journeys. Surround yourself with people who can offer support, advice, and encouragement when you need it.

Confidence in your financial future also comes from having a safety net. Building an emergency fund, as mentioned earlier, is a great way to protect yourself from life's unexpected events without dipping into your retirement savings. Knowing that you have a cushion for those "just in case" moments will help you sleep better at night.

And finally, keep the big picture in mind. It's easy to get bogged down in the details of financial planning, but remember why you're doing this. Retirement is about more than just numbers on a spreadsheet—it's about creating the freedom to live your best life, pursue your passions, and spend time with the people you love. When you focus on the ultimate goal—a secure and fulfilling retirement—you'll find that the small financial decisions you make along the way become easier, and your confidence will naturally grow.

In the end, your personalized action plan isn't just about reaching financial milestones. It's about building a foundation that allows you to live the life you've dreamed of, with the peace of mind that comes from knowing you're financially prepared. By taking it one step at a time, sticking to the plan, and adjusting as needed, you'll be well on your way to a successful retirement that truly reflects your hopes and aspirations. Remember, retirement is not just a destination; it's a journey that unfolds over time, and with a solid action plan in place, you can navigate this journey with confidence and joy.

As you embark on this exciting new chapter of life, embrace the opportunity to discover new passions and deepen existing relationships. Retirement can open doors you never even considered, and with your financial future secure, you can focus on what truly matters to you. Whether that means volunteering in your community, picking up a long-lost hobby, or spending more time with family, the possibilities are endless.

Don't forget to celebrate your milestones along the way, no matter how small they may seem. Each step you take toward your retirement goals is a victory that deserves recognition. Whether it's finally reaching that savings target, securing a part-time gig that excites you, or simply enjoying a leisurely day free from work obligations, take a moment to acknowledge your progress. These celebrations help keep your spirits high and reinforce the positive mindset that is essential for enjoying your retirement.

Additionally, as you prepare to embrace this new lifestyle, consider the power of adaptability. Life is full of surprises, and the ability to pivot when necessary is crucial for a fulfilling retirement. Be open to new experiences and willing to learn from them. Whether you find yourself drawn to a new passion, shifting your spending habits, or exploring different retirement locales, embracing change can lead to unexpected joys and opportunities.

It's also important to stay connected with your community. Building social connections and engaging with others who share similar interests can enrich your retirement experience and enhance your emotional well-being. Join clubs, take classes, or participate in local events that resonate with your passions. Not only will you make new friends, but you'll also create a support network that can be invaluable as you navigate retirement.

Lastly, remember that your retirement is uniquely yours. Resist the urge to compare yourself to others or feel pressured to conform to societal expectations of what retirement should look like. Everyone's journey is different, and your retirement should reflect your values, interests, and dreams. Trust in your personalized action plan and the hard work you've put into preparing for this moment.

As you move forward, keep your mind open and your heart engaged. Retirement is an adventure waiting to unfold, and with your plan in place, you're ready to make the most of it. Life after work can be richer and more fulfilling than you ever imagined, filled with excitement, exploration, and newfound freedom. So, gear up, embrace your new lifestyle, and remember that the best is yet to come. Happy retirement!